9/18

JUNIOR
BIOGRAPHIES

MELANIA TRUMP

FIRST LADY OF THE UNITED STATES

Enslow Publishing
101 ...
Suite ...
New ...
USA ...

Kristen Rajczak Nelson

WORDS TO KNOW

architecture The art and science of making plans for buildings.

convention A large gathering of people to discuss their work and make decisions.

green card A paper that says a citizen of another country can legally work and live in the United States.

imperative An important duty.

independent Not ruled by another country; able to stand on one's own.

influence The power to affect someone or something.

naturalize To become a new citizen.

nomination The act of choosing someone to run for a position or job.

pattern A plan that is followed to make a piece of clothing.

work visa The official paper that allows a citizen of another country to work in the United States for a certain period of time.

CONTENTS

Melania Trump

First Lady of the United States Melania Trump was born Melanija Knavs on April 26, 1970. She was born in Novo Mesto, Slovenia, a country in eastern Europe. Slovenia was part of Yugoslavia at the time. Melania and her sister, Ines, mostly grew up in the town of Sevnica, which was on the Sava River.

Melania's father, Viktor, was a driver for a local mayor. He later sold cars. Melania's mother, Amalija, was a big **influence** on her. She worked at a factory making **patterns** for children's clothing. In her spare time, Amalija would sew clothing for herself and two daughters. She wanted the girls to be dressed well.

Melania Says:

"I always liked myself. Even when other kids teased me, I didn't care. I knew what I wanted to do. I found my passion at such an early age. It helped with my confidence."

A GOOD STUDENT

Melania liked school and worked hard at her studies as a child. She enjoyed art classes and was good at drawing. She even began designing her own clothing that her mother and sister made. People who knew Melania as a child said she was quiet and shy. By the time she was a teenager, she was also very tall and beautiful.

As a child, Melania lived in this apartment block in Sevnica, Slovenia.

Melania's mother traveled to other countries in Europe for work. She would bring home fashion magazines that Melania loved to look at over and over again.

Melania's parents, Victor and Amalija Knavs

A YOUNG BEAUTY

In 1987, when Melania was about seventeen, a photographer saw her while she was out with some friends. He asked if she wanted to do a photo shoot with him. Soon after, she did. These would be Melania's very first modeling photos. However, at that time, she wanted to focus more on studying at the Secondary School of Design and Photography in the bigger city of Ljubljana, Slovenia.

CHAPTER 2
MODEL BEHAVIOR

After her first photo shoot, Melania started taking a few modeling classes through a local cultural center. She also started attending college at the University of Ljubljana. She planned to study architecture. Melania didn't stay in college there very long, though. She soon left to try and work as a model full time.

In 1992, Melania entered a modeling contest put on by a Slovenian women's magazine called *Jana*. Winning the contest could really help a Slovenian model's career. Those who came in the top three would earn modeling contracts in Europe. Melania ended up coming in second.

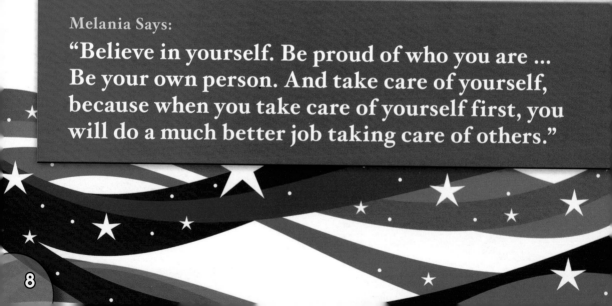

Melania Says:

"Believe in yourself. Be proud of who you are ... Be your own person. And take care of yourself, because when you take care of yourself first, you will do a much better job taking care of others."

Once Melania began her career as a model, she traveled around Europe for photo shoots.

ON THE MOVE

The same year, Slovenia became **independent** from Yugolsavia. Suddenly, Melania's country had fewer people and fewer opportunities for modeling work. So, she took her success in the contest and moved to Milan, Italy. Over the next few years, Melania modeled in many places in Europe, including Paris, France. During this time, she changed the spelling of her name from "Knavs" to "Knauss" and dropped the "j" in her first name.

Melania has appeared in many magazines, including *Sports Illustrated, Glamour, Vanity Fair,* and *Vogue.*

AMERICAN OPPORTUNITY

Melania was doing well in her work in Europe. But, when Paolo Zampolli, the founder of a modeling company in the United States, offered to bring her to New York City, she went. She received a modeling contact and a work visa. This move would change Melania's life, both personally and as a model.

In 1996, Melania moved to New York City to pursue her modeling career.

CHAPTER 3
MEETING DONALD

In 1998, Melania went to a party Paolo was holding. Also invited was wealthy businessman Donald Trump. Donald spotted Melania from across the party and wanted to meet her. Melania said he was "charming" when they met. Not long after, they became a couple. Both Melania and Donald say they are a good fit for one another. One friend said Melania is a "calming influence" on Donald. Melania often says one reason their relationship works is that she doesn't want to change Donald. They have independent lives away from one another.

Melania Says:

"We are both very independent—I let him be who he is and he lets me be who I am."

When Melania met Donald Trump, she was twenty-eight and he was fifty-two.

Melania and Donald pose with, from left, his daughter, Ivanka, daughter-in-law, Vanessa, and son, Donald Jr.

BIG CHANGES

The early 2000s were a busy time for Melania and Donald. In 2000, Donald considered running for US president. Melania received her **green card** in 2001. Then, after a big party in April 2004, Donald asked Melania to marry him. Donald had been married twice before, but Melania was sure that their relationship would last.

Donald and Melania got married on January 22, 2005, at Donald's home called Mar-a-Lago in Palm Beach, Florida. Many famous people came to the wedding, including Hillary and Bill Clinton, Usher, Arnold Schwarzenegger, and Shaquille O'Neal.

NEW FAMILY

In 2006, Melania was **naturalized** as a US citizen. She and Donald also welcomed a son, Barron, on March 20, 2006. He was Melania's first child and Donald's fifth. Much of the

Melania holds young Barron in 2007.

Melania speaks Slovenian, French, and Italian, in addition to English. She taught her son Slovenian so he could speak with his grandparents.

time, the new Trump family lived together in New York City in Trump Tower. Melania was proud to stay home and take care of her son herself as much as she could. After Barron was born, Melania's parents also came to live in New York for a time to help with their grandson.

Once Barron started school, Melania started her own business. In 2010, Melania's jewelry line came out on QVC, a TV and online shopping network. Still, she has called being Barron's mom "the most important job ever." Even though she had meetings and other duties, she made sure to spend as much time with her son as she could.

THE ROAD TO THE WHITE HOUSE

In June 2015, Donald announced that he would run for president. Melania encouraged his decision. She said she believed he would be a great leader for the United States. However, she didn't spend much time working on

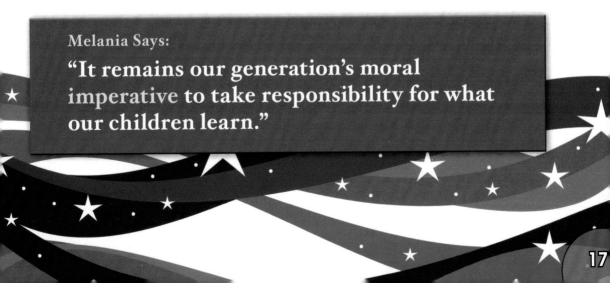

Melania Says:

"It remains our generation's moral imperative to take responsibility for what our children learn."

Melania and Barron enjoy a screening of *The Lego Movie* in 2014.

the campaign. Instead, she stayed with Barron to make sure his life stayed mostly normal. Melania did speak at the Republican National Convention in July 2016. There, Donald won the Republication nomination for president. Just four months later, Donald won the presidential election.

A NEW LIFE

Though Melania became the First Lady, she still believed her first job is to be Barron's mother. She and Barron didn't move into the White House until months after Donald took office. Melania didn't want their son to have to change schools in the middle of the year.

Melania is only the second First Lady ever to have been born outside of the United States. The other was Louisa Adams, the wife of John Quincy Adams, the sixth president. She was born in London, England.

Melania delivers a speech at the Republican National Convention in 2016.

Donald and Melania host Canadian prime minister Justin Trudeau and his wife, Sophie, at the White House in 2017.

In New York City, Melania had been a part of many charities that work to raise money to help children in need. As First Lady, it's likely Melania will continue to work on similar causes. She is interested in working against bullying, and with her strong, independent spirit, US citizens have a lot to look forward to!

TIMELINE

1970 Melanija Knavs is born on April 26 in the country formerly known as Yugoslavia.

1987 Does her first photo shoot as a model.

1996 Moves to New York City.

1998 Meets Donald Trump at a party.

2005 Marries Donald.

2006 Barron Trump is born.
Melania becomes an official US citizen.

2010 Releases her own jewelry line on QVC.

2017 Becomes First Lady of the United States.

LEARN MORE

BOOKS

Bryan, Bethany. *Melania Trump: The Model Who Became First Lady*. New York, NY: Cavendish Square Publishing, 2018.

DK. *First Ladies*. New York, NY: DK Publishing, 2017.

Nagelhout, Ryan. *Before Donald Trump Was President*. New York, NY: Gareth Stevens Publishing, 2018.

WEBSITES

The First Ladies at the Smithsonian
americanhistory.si.edu/first-ladies/introduction
Learn more about other First Ladies through the Smithsonian exhibition.

First Lady Melania Trump
www.whitehouse.gov/administration/first-lady-melania-trump
Visit Melania's official White House biography page.

Index

Published in 2019 by Enslow Publishing, LLC.
101 W. 23rd Street, Suite 240, New York, NY 10011

Library of Congress Cataloging-in-Publication Data
Names: Rajczak Nelson, Kristen, author.
Title: Melania Trump : First Lady of the United States / Kristen Rajczak Nelson.
Description: New York: Enslow Publishing, 2019. | Series: Junior biographies | Includes bibliographical references and index. | Audience: Grades 3-6.
Identifiers: LCCN 2017047223| ISBN 9780766097391 (library bound) | ISBN 9780766097407 (pbk.) | ISBN 9780766097414 (6 pack)
Subjects: LCSH: Trump, Melania–Juvenile literature. | Presidents' spouses–United States–Biography–Juvenile literature.
Classification: LCC E914.T77 R34 2019 | DDC 973.933092 [B] –dc23
LC record available at https://lccn.loc.gov/2017047223
Printed in the United States of America

To Our Readers: We have done our best to make sure all website addresses in this book were active and appropriate when we went to press. However, the author and the publisher have no control over and assume no liability for the material available on those websites or on any websites they may link to. Any comments or suggestions can be sent by e-mail to customerservice@enslow.com.

Photos Credits: Cover, p. 1 The White House/Getty Images; p. 4 John Lamparski/WireImage/Getty Images; p. 6 Jack Taylor/Getty Images; p. 7 Chris Kleponis Pool via CNP/Newscom; p. 9 Diane Freed/Hulton Archive/Getty Images; p. 11 New York Daily News Archive/Getty Images; p. 13 Ron Galella Collection/Getty Images; p. 14 Patrick McMullan/Getty Images; p. 15 Jamie McCarthy/WireImage/Getty Images; p. 18 Ben Gabbe/FilmMagic/Getty Images; p. 20 Robyn Beck/AFP/Getty Images; p. 21 The Washington Post/Getty Images; back cover, pp. 2, 3, 22, 23, 24 (curves graphic) Alena Kazlouskaya/Shutterstock.com; interior page bottoms (stars and stripes) Tharun 15/Shutterstock.com.